TEOTIHUACAN

INSTITUTO NACIONAL DE ANTROPOLOGIA E HISTORIA
  GENERAL DIRECTOR
  Arqglo. Roberto García Moll

DIRECTION OF PREHISPANIC MONUMENTS
  Ing. Joaquín García Bárcena

PUBLICATIONS DIRECTOR
  Jaime Bali Wuest

SALVAT MEXICANA DE EDICIONES, S.A. DE C.V.

GENERAL DIRECTOR
  Lic. Leopoldo Escobar Z.

EDITORIAL CO-ORDINATOR
  Ma. Del Carmen Tejero

DESIGN AND ILUSTRATION
  Josefina González de la Vara
  Alberto Rodríguez
  Patricia Rubio

FOTOGRAPHY
  Alejandro Mass
  Salvat Files

TRADUCTION
  Helen Jones-Perrott de Mandri

1985, First edition
1988, First reimpression

PRINTED IN 1988 by:
  Gráficas Monte Albán, S.A. de C.V.
  Municipio El Marqués, Querétaro.

  Impreso en México
  Printed in Mexico

RIGHTS RESERVED ©
  Instituto Nacional de Antropología e Historia
  Salvat Mexicana de Ediciones, S.A. de C.V.
  ISBN 968-32-0344-2

  This reimpression consists
  of 3,500 copies plus additionals.

OFFICIAL GUIDE

TEOTIHUACAN

Original Text
DR. IGNACIO BERNAL

Text excavations 1964 to present
ARCHAEOLOGIST RUBEN CABRERA

INAH-SALVAT

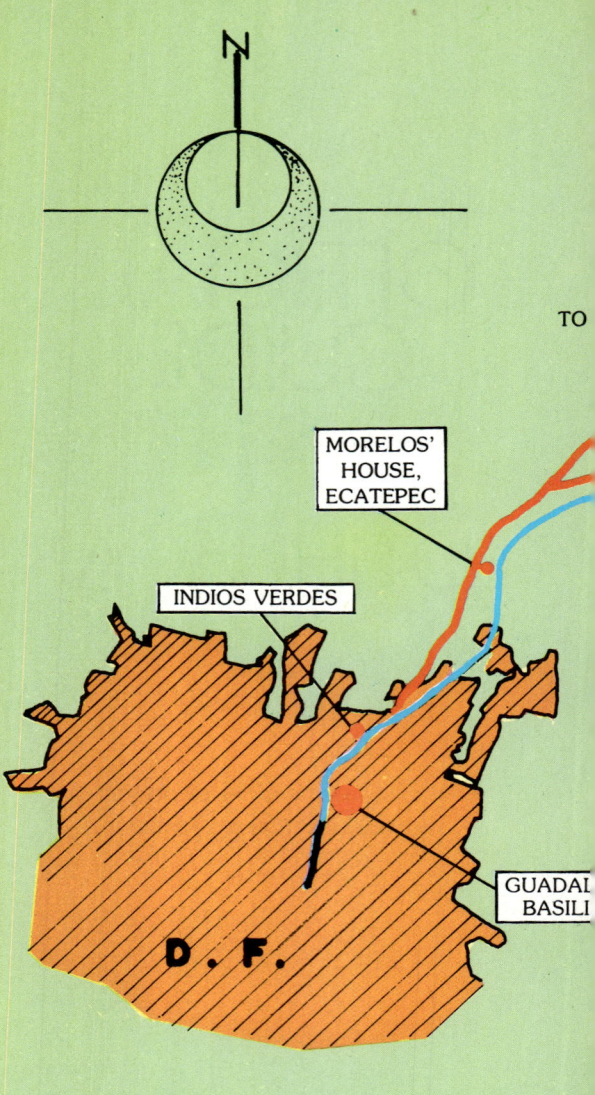

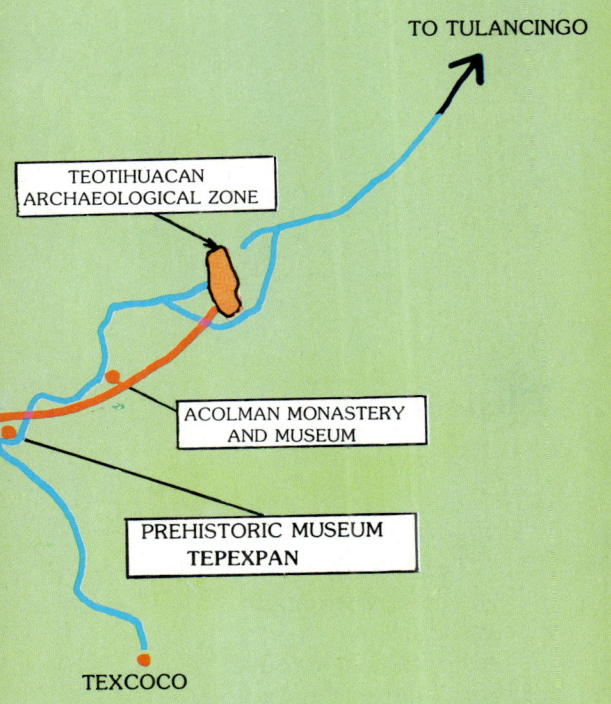

MAP SHOWING ACCESS TO TEOTIHUACAN

Contents

Map showing access to Teotihuacan	4
General Information	7
Introduction	9
Historical Background	10
Teotihuacan Chronology	12
Mural Painting	26
Buildings and Districts	33
Peak Development	37
Political Change	40
City Planning and Society	43
Influence in Mesoamerica	47
The End of Metropolitan Teotihuacan	51
The Living Mythical and Historical Teotihuacan	58
Archaeology in Teotihuacan	64
A Tour of Teotihuacan	66
The Museum	68
The Citadel	69
The Street of the Dead	83
Plaza 2	86
Northwest Complex	89

The Street of the Dead Complex	90
The Superimposed Buildings	92
The West Plaza Complex	95
The Viking Group	100
The Plaza of the Sun	100
The Pyramid of the Sun	101
Four Small Temples	105
Mythical Animals	106
Temple of Agriculture	108
The Plaza of the Moon	109
The Pyramid of the Moon	112
The Palace of the Quetzal-Butterfly	112
The Jaguar Palace	115
Substructure of the Plumed Conch-Shells	118
Tepantitla	121
Atetelco	128
Tetitla	131
Zacuala	135
Yayahuala	135

GENERAL INFORMATION

Hours:
>Museum and Archaeological Zone.
>Daily from 8:00 a.m. to 5:00 p.m.

Admission:
>Entrance is not expensive.
>Students and Teachers with I.D. FREE.
>There are 5 entrances to the Archaeological Zone.

Performance:
>LIGHT AND SOUND.
>Tuesday through Sunday.
>7:00 p.m. in English
>8:15 p.m. in Spanish.

Admission:
>Entrance by Gate Number 3.
>Tickets on sale from 6:30 p.m. hours.

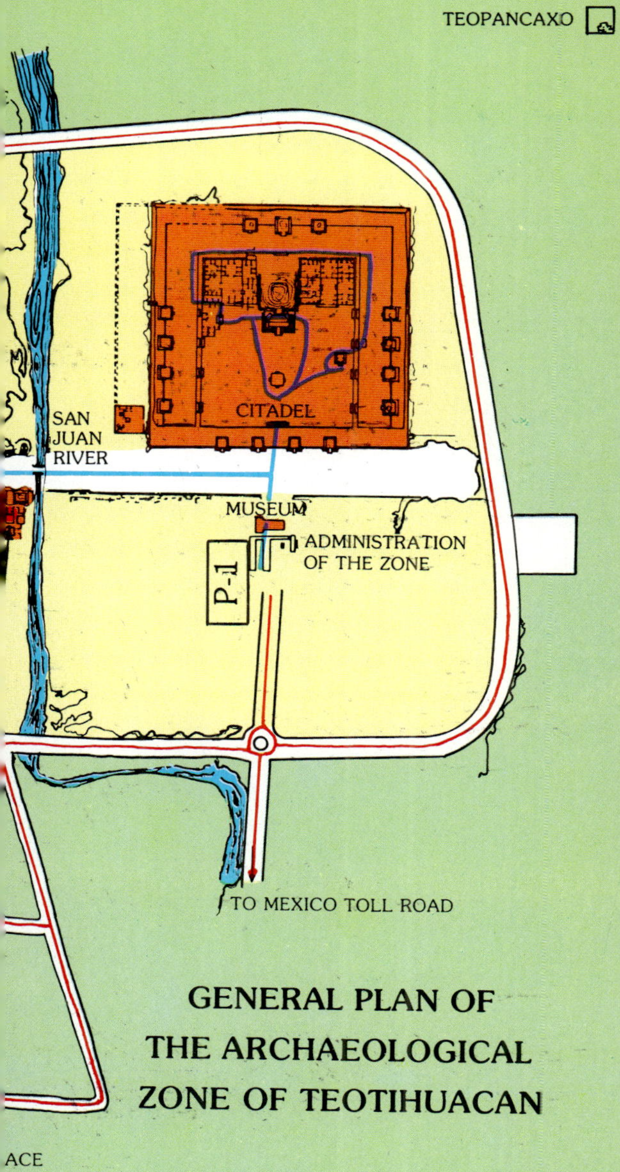

TEOPANCAXO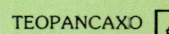

SAN JUAN RIVER

CITADEL

MUSEUM

P-1

ADMINISTRATION OF THE ZONE

TO MEXICO TOLL ROAD

GENERAL PLAN OF THE ARCHAEOLOGICAL ZONE OF TEOTIHUACAN

INTRODUCTION

A visit to Teotihuacan is imperative for anyone wishing to understand Mexico, not only to become acquainted with the largest ruins of ancient America, the splendid planning and serene harmony of its structures as a whole, but also because, we can say that, in a way, the history of Mexico begins here. It is here that the cultural, political, economic, and religious traditions were formed that would mark the path that subsequent cultures in the two great valleys of the Central Plateau, would follow. For the first and only time in Prehispanic history, the Mexico and Puebla valleys were united under one rule.

The triumph of Teotihuacan more than 2,000 years ago, transformed the Central Plateau forever into the dominant region of Mexico. This event influenced her entire history.

Just as Teotihuacan's fascination attracts tourists and scholars of today and makes it an obligatory visit, its fame made it a center for devout pilgrimages of yesterday. Everyone wished to come and implore favors of these omnipotent gods who had created such majesty and splendor. It was for centuries the Rome and Mecca of Precolumbian history.

Despite numerous explorations carried out in the city —which we will visit later on— and the gathering of a considerable amount of information which contributes to the enormous task of trying to reconstruct its past, we are still left with a sketchy outline of what it might have been. The site has left us the legacy of its magnificent ruins but not a single written word. The little that was recorded by later peoples are merely legends, more like the adventures of gods than the history of men.

But first of all, let's take a general look at the different eras of this reconstructed history that correspond to the birth, development, splendor, decadence and end of the city.

HISTORICAL BACKGROUND

Our still incomplete knowledge indicates that towards the middle of the first millenium before Christ, the region that Teotihuacan would later occupy was populated by various small farming villages similar to others which were scattered over the Central Plateu. The cultural level of these villages corresponded to the

The *Avenue of the Dead Complex,* located next to the north-south axis of the urban center of Teotihuacan, gives us an idea of the living areas of the inhabitants of Teotihuacan.

final stages of the Preclassical period of the area. In some sites, such as Cuicuilco, important centers had been built portending future developments.

The number of inhabitants of all the villages together, in what would later become the city, could not have exceeded the modest figure of 1,000 individuals; while in the entire Teotihuacan Valley, where there were 25 more villages, the total population was no greater than 5,000 to 6,000 inhabitants.

In the second century before Christ, a larger settlement began to form in the western part of the present city. This quickly grew until it covered an area of 2½ square miles and eventually reached 7,000 inhabitants. The houses

CHRONOLOGY

DATE CHRISTIAN ERA	PHASE	POPULATION	AREA Square Miles	SOCIO-ECONOMIC MANIFESTATIONS
				CLASSIC
900-600 A.D.	Teotihuacán IV	60,000 inhabitants.	8	Crisis and decadence, disappearance of tributary for...
600-300 A.D.	Teotihuacán III	200,000 inhabitants.	8	Tribute and commerce ba... of the Teotihuac... economy.
300-150 A.D.	Teotihuacán II	45,000 - 50,000 inhabitants	8	Intensive agricultural ac... ties, important commer... relations and tributaries.
				PRECLASSIC
150 A.D. to 100 B.C.	Teotihuacán I	25,000 - 20,000 inhabitants	8	Work and wide commerc... obsidian.
100 - 200 B.C.		7,000 inhabitants.	2½	Obsidian Exploitation.
200 - 2000		10,000		

were grouped in small, somewhat dispersed nuclei, which were possibly families. It was then that a transformation began which was to lead to the birth of a city. It is possible that from the start, these hamlets exploited the obsidian mines located in the surrounding hills and thus were able to supply raw material to a few workshops that produced implements from it. So, as early as this, commerce in this volcanic glass appeared, and it was exported to ever more distant places. Although we still cannot speak of any large permanent build-

TEOTIHUACAN

POLITICAL MANIFESTATIONS	CONSTRUCTION ACTIVITY	BUILDINGS
PERIOD		
...integration of the State ...d social crisis. Influence ...appears. Decadence.	No building construction, the beginning of the Destruction.	No more building.
...itia and civilians join the ...ate with the priests who ...re the most influential in ...otihuacán.	End of great complex. Height of urban activity.	All the great buildings are finished.
...nsolidation of Teotihua-...n State marked Teotihua-...n influence in ...soamérica.	Beginning of climax of mural painting large monolithic sculptures.	Pyramid of the Sun finished and Pyramid of the Moon enlarged. Pyramid of Quetzalcoatl.
PERIOD		
...e State emerges. Division ...the society into social ...ses.	Tremendous construction activity. Teotihuacán becomes an urban center.	Avenue of the Dead, Pyramids of the Sun and Moon, city divided into 4 quarters.
...bal Organization.	Nuclei of Villages.	Stone houses.

ing, material remains that have been found here and there do indicate at least a partial human settlement.

Thus the course was set that would lead Teotihuacan to become a sacred city. The area for the building of the Pyramid of the Sun, which belongs to the next phase, was not chosen by accident but because of the fact that an ancient cave existed there, which had been converted into a modest sanctuary in the remote past.

TEOTIHUACAN I

Shortly before the time of Christ, the phase we call Teotihuacan I began.

In about 250 to 300 years, the city expanded to cover an area of 8 square miles, and its population increased to 25,000 to 30,000 inhabitants, unevenly distributed among various areas. The building activity was astonishing: we know of 23 building complexes along the Avenue of the Dead alone. This shows that by then, the splendid central axis which was the pride of the city had already been defined. It is possible that the east and west avenues, extending almost in a right angle from the central avenue, were also from this period. They cross more or less at the point where

The *Pyramid of the Moon,* at the north end of the Avenue of the Dead, clearly demonstrates the monumental use of urban space in Teotihuacan.

the so-called Citadel is located. This suggests that the nucleus of the future ceremonial center was by then already established. This means that from this stage on, the city was divided into four large quarters, a very interesting feature of urban planning that Tenochtitlan was to inherit more than a thousand years later. In addition, the Avenue of the Dead was extended a further 1¼ miles to the south until it probably reached some 2½ miles in total length.

The largest structures in Teotihuacan were built precisely in this first phase. The monumental volume of the Pyramid of the Sun was built and also the interior of the Pyramid of the Moon which was completed at a later date. Teotihuacan had by now become the main center for the Valley of Mexico.

There has been considerable discussion over whether Teotihuacan, like various other Mesoamerican sites, was really a city in the sense that we understand it now, or simply a ceremonial center. That is, was it a place where the temples to the gods were situat-

Huhueteotl, the ancient god of fire, one of the first gods to be recognized in the Mesoamerican pantheon.

ed, where the priests and political hierarchy lived, and where, consequently, some administrative centers were to be found, but where the main populace did not live, instead

being scattered in the surrounding villages and towns? This old idea, probably valid for some of the sites in the Mayan area, is certainly impossible to maintain today when referring to Teotihuacan.

From the first phase on, Teotihuacan was a city in the universal sense, and not merely a Mesoamerican ceremonial center. In other words, from that moment on, all the elements of an urban civilization, the only kind of civilization that has ever existed in the world, were present. I say urban, in the true meaning of the word, which means, not only a relative agglomeration of people in one place, but also the definite and complex division of social classes: there are diverse leaders with their numerous and varied subordinates; there are rich and poor; and in consequence, the need for professionals in various employments and above all, a government run on lines that in no way resemble those of a tribal system.

In phase I of Teotihuacan, the urban world had already dominated the primitive world. There was specialization and professionalism in work which implied architects, sculptors, painters, potters, stonemasons, farmers, priests, and officials.

The last of these sectors, priests and officials, formed a coherent ruling force. This division by professions, by jobs and activities, is the fundamental characteristic of any urban society. These were already apparent in Teotihuacan by this first phase, though perhaps not as strikingly as in the following phases; still, they undoubtedly existed. We cannot consider for even a moment, that such exact planning implied by the tall pyramids and the layout of the long avenues at right angles could be executed without the existence of a planning organism which could control the people from building in their former disorderly fashion. Rather, they must have followed a plan indicated by a previously established order, as we do in our own cities today.

We can say the same of the architecture. The building of these colossal masses was not credible of people in a pre-urban civilization. They would not have had the technical knowledge nor the human capacity to do it. All this implies that the transformation from a tribal to an urban way of life was already well established.

Tlaloc, the rain god, is the principal deity of Teotihuacan. The continued existence of the city and the harvests depended on him.

In the Valley of Mexico, the rivers are insignificant, if they exist at all; the annual quantity of rainfall is, from the farming point of view, not so much insufficient but poorly distributed; the winter frosts are severe and kill the crops: in other words, the natural conditions do not seem to favor a great development. However, there were lakes, which the Teotihuacan people took full advantage of in a thousand ways, as did the later Mexicas. These exceedingly abundant lakes provided infinite benefits: not only fish and other aquatic animals, but also the facility of canoe transport and the possibility of irrigating their land.

I believe this is precisely what the Teotihuacan people did. To begin with, this irrigation must have taken place simply at the edge of the lake. The level of the lake would have risen in the rainy season and dropped with the winter drought, leaving a coastal area that would flood and dry up periodically. This area, narrow but long, was opened up to allow much richer and more productive crops than any that could grow on the rather dry lands of the plateau.

The Valley of Teotihuacan, like many other regions of Mexico, shows unquestionable evidence of two other systems that were used

Sculpture of a jaguar head from the West Plaza Complex. It originally decorated the sloping masonry encasements of the stairways, an architectonic feature reproduced in subsequent cities, including Tenochtitlan, which the Spaniards admired so much.

to increase the productivity of the land: irrigation by canals and terracing, which would increase the available agricultural surface. However, the problem is that we are not sure if the irrigation canals and terraces correspond to the first period of Teotihuacan. There has been much discussion on the matter and, though it is certain that both systems existed, their dates are not exact. Another similar case in agriculture is that of the *chinampas* (small man-made tracts of land constructed in the lakes), which, though found within the region, may possibly correspond to a later period than when the great city flourished.

Be that as it may, Teotihuacan already had a work force at her disposal sufficient to cope with her daily affairs and even a surplus of unemployed manpower that permitted the building of enormous edifices which were of no direct economic interest.

Evidently, there were other products, natural or manufactured, with which Teotihuacan began to trade. The most important product,

The Pyramid of the Sun, which together with Cholula, is the largest building in Prehispanic Mexico.

or at least the one that has left the most traces, is obsidian, which we mentioned earlier, and which appears to have been widely developed during this period.

Archaeological exploration also shows that Teotihuacan was evolving more and more into a religious center of major importance. The very existence of the Pyramid of the Sun which had practically reached its full height in the first phase, is undoubtable proof of the strength and power of the city as a sacred center. Perhaps it was not only the city dwellers, but also people from the valley that helped in its building. perhaps it was for the same reason, that the Valley of Mexico suffered a notable decrease in population due to the emigration of many of its inhabitants to the great city which rapidly increased its popula-

tion. Nevertheless, Teotihuacan managed to control and order this emigration. This fact surely accelerated the formation of the Teotihuacan State, which is only understandable given the existence of an advanced and flexible social system.

TEOTIHUACAN II

Important as all this might be, it was really only a prelude. From 150 A. D., when Phase II began, Teotihuacan took another step forward. The constructed area of the city did not increase further and in fact, did not grow during the following periods, but it did almost double its population and it eventually reached between 45,000 and 50,000 inhabitants. This was accomplished by filling the vacant plots with numerous constructions for housing and services.

During Phase II, the summit of the Pyramid of the Sun was finished, with the structure that

Relief of a quetzal-bird with precious feathers, which decorates one of the columns in the Palace of the Quetzal-Butterfly, belonging to one of the Teotihuacan nobles.

we see today and the penultimate reconstruction of the summit of Pyramid of the Moon was also completed. Undoubtedly, many other buildings were constructed during this period but the most impressive was the Temple of Quetzalcoatl, one of the greatest triumphs of the Teotihuacan architects.

These buildings and others belong to a new

The *Palace of* the Quetzal-Butterfly, a good example of the residences of the Teotihuacan leaders.

architectural style, with pyramidal platforms on which alternate sloping *taluds* and upright *tableros* repeated until the desired height was reached. At that time, all monuments were built of stone and coated with lime, which in a number of cases permitted painted mural decorations. Therefore, the stone completely disappeared from human view, and what we now see as ochre stone ruins were, for the

Mural painting was a highly developed artistic expression of the Teotihuacan artisans. It helps to bring us closer to the ancient inhabitants of the ancient city.

inhabitants of those days, resplendent monuments in vivid colors.

Both the outside and inside frescoes, depict scenes sometimes of incredible beauty. The number of murals would multiply in the following centuries. And it seems that they are still enjoyed by present-day Mexicans...

MURAL PAINTING

TEOTIHUACAN III

The abundance of mural paintings produced during Teotihuacan Phase III is extraordinary. In no other Mesoamerican site are there so many painted walls. There is hardly a wall

27

This *mural* painting shows the Teotihuacan artists skillfulness using line and color.

without a fresco: not only the interior walls and courtyards but also the exterior facades. Not only because of their quantity, but also because of their quality, the Teotihuacan paintings mark the zenith of this art in the Central Plateau of Mexico.

Indigenous painting basically consisted of line drawings in red and black and filled in with flat colors. There was no perspective or

shading. Distances were indicated by the positioning of the more distant objects above the nearer objects which were placed in the lower part of the composition. But, for very different reasons, the size of human figures and objects representd did not follow this simple rule of perspective. It was necessary to indicate the relative importance of each figure and this was achieved by giving a greater size —sometimes very exaggerated— to those who were most important.

Although all the painting has religious symbolism, we can distinguish various different styles among the subject matter found in Teotihuacan. There are those we might call the great representations of deities and officials, whether they be gods or priests dressed almost as gods. In that case, they wear the most complicated of headdresses, vestments full of ornaments and a large number of jewels. They are always celebrating a ritual ceremony, to which the god has already responded. Thus, for example, we see that drops of rain or a series of objects painted green (indicating that they are made of jade and symbolize the rain that waters the fields) fall from the hands of the

Tlaloc, **the great Teotihuacan rain god, in the Tlalocan mural.**

rain god, resulting from the prayers of the faithful. They are like hieroglyphs with an esoteric meaning, and in that sense like prayers. Their object was not directly artistic; the beauty is mainly accidental; what is important is the religious symbolism.

There is also a large number of paintings showing animals, sometimes real, sometimes mythical. There are animals of every possible kind, some taken from nature, others non-existent in reality. They show magical concepts that often combine two animals in one element. Quetzalcoatl is, of course, the most famous of all; no one has ever seen a serpent with feathers and yet, we find this motif frequently represented. Animals in a terrible battle

contrast with others who file serenely before our eyes, and we are surprised to see jaguars as gentle as lambs.

There is another entirely different group which is much more abstract, without human or zoomorphic reference. At first glance, there are no real or recognizable objects and it is even more like a hieroglyphic writing which is difficult for us to understand, but at the time, it must have been intelligible, at least to the priests.

There are also other paintings whose object is purely decorative, as in some of the friezes adorned with plants and flowers which frame human or animal motifs.

Finally, there are some rather more realistic and descriptive frescoes, even though they also contain symbolic elements. Among these, is the scene of the *Tlalocan* from Tepantitla

Large sculpture of *Tlaloc* from a Coatlinchan quarry, apparently destined for the Pyramid of the Sun, but never finished. It can now been seen at the entrance to the National Anthropology Museum.

which we will see further along, or the fresco of 'the offering to the gods, unfortunately now disappeared, of which we only preserve a more or less exact copy.

Buildings and districts

Monumental, monolithic sculptures, such as the Goddess of Water and Tlaloc, the sculpted facades of the Temple of Quetzalcoatl and the facade which has how disappeared, at the base of the Pyramid of the Sun, were already being carved in Phase II.

The city's enormous progress is not only evident in its public buildings. In many places, the old, modest houses were replaced by vast compounds resembling apartments with stone walls and wood-beamed terrace roofs. The nature of these compounds, which were ob-

Female sculpture that **shows the type of dress worn by the Teotihuacan women, with a quechquemetl (triangular overblouse) and underskirt. (National Anthropology Museum).**

The *West Plaza Complex* (above) and the *Northeast Complex* (below) both flanking the *Avenue of the Dead,* show us the architectural pattern used in the Teotihuacan residential units, with the rooms distributed around plazas.

viously residential, is still something of a mystery to us. At times they were thought to be palaces, which would be the correct name if we were talking about the dwelling of some

34

Tripod vessel with lid, from Teotihuacan Phase III (National Anthropology Museum). It is made of a fine, orange-colored earthenware, a commercial material widely distributed within the Teotihuacan sphere.

dignitary, but the majority are groups of rooms with a division between each group, indicating that they might have been apartments, each inhabited by a family. Perhaps the families were

Detail of a painted tripod vessel. The Teotihuacan III ceramic is orange-colored and delicate, with decorative painting and reliefs.

related to each other by blood or tribal ties, and they formed a group with their own temple situated within the communal courtyard.

The districts were clearly defined by the specialized work of the residents, or by their regional origin. Thus there were districts of people dedicated to making pottery or figurines, or to carving obsidian objects. We have found workshops of potters, stonemasons, craftsmen in materials such as shell or slate, bricklayers, and plasterers. There are many others who have left no trace, but one can imagine them, judging by those that we have found.

The foreing districts, typical of any metropolis, are very interesting. The most obvious one in Teotihuacan, is of people coming from the Valley of Oaxaca. It even contains a tomb in the style of Monte Alban.

PEAK DEVELOPMENT

Between the beginning of the 1st century after Christ and the middle of the 7th, throughout Teotihuacan Phase III, the development in construction achieved its supreme heights. The main buildings begun in ancient times were finished, together with the Pyramid in the Plaza of the Moon which is the most beautiful of all the marvellous squares of ancient America, surrounded by serene buildings. Teotihuacan passed through a period which Dr. Millon has called "an urban renewal", because, from then on, the apartments were mainly built

The *Pyramid of the Moon.* Here we see the characteristic features of the Teotihuacan platforms with the alternating framed *tableros* (upright panels) and *taluds* (inclined panels).

The *Plaza of the Moon* with its principal element, the pyramid, surrounded by temple platforms, was the focal point of the city.

of stone and plaster, bordered by narrow streets in an aproximately square lay-out. This Teotihuacan architectural system seems to have been unique in Mesoamerica.

Now the great metropolis had reached full activity, with its magnificent civic and religious center which was situated in the Citadel and the great open space in front of it. Surrounding it, were the main houses and the many, clearly defined districts.

When I spoke earlier of the planning, I

referred both to the axis of the two avenues that form a cross and to the place and moment in time which was the point of departure for the constructions which we now call the "great complex". In fact, only a relatively small section of what once existed is visible to today's visitor, as the greatest part has not been sufficiently explored. The "great complex" seems to have been, from the moment of its construction, the center of the city, that is, its administrative and religious axis. The interesting thing about the "great complex" and this four-part division of the city, is that it was to be exactly reproduced in Tenochtitlan.

POLITICAL CHANGE

At this time there was an immensely important event, which unfortunately is, as yet, difficult to decipher clearly, and which produced a fundamental change.

Secular officials, be they military or civilian, now took part in the decisions of a government which turned its vision more to this world of men and less to the mystical. Now they were the ones to impose their ideas. They were more interested naturally in the area of housing and their palaces than in the great temples dedi-

Platform with the sloping masonry stairway encasements decorated with serpent heads. *Avenue of the Dead Complex.*

cated to the gods. It is not that the priests lost their prestige, but at this stage, they were not the only ones to take a dominant role. The "great complex" was completed, made up of this religious and civic combination, in addition to its commercial function which has already been mentioned. It was from this period on that a significant political transformation occurred. The human concentration gave rise to the need to create this magnificent civic and theocratic epicenter. Teotihuacan would no longer be guided only by the priests, who, after all, created its grandeur, but would turn into something definitely secular, much more dedicated to humanity, just as the tall pyramids had been dedicated to the gods.

The area did not increase, but the number of dwellings multiplied and became more crowded and it is probable that they contained some 200,000 inhabitants.

CITY PLANNING AND SOCIETY

City planning changed radically with the pressure of a large number of inhabitants in a limited area. The city became compact with no vacant spaces except, of course, those wide avenues and ceremonial squares. Innumerable little streets opened up, virtual alleyways dividing one building from another, typical of all crowded cities. The rooms of the houses were surrounded by other apartments, without however, losing the essential element of the central patio. This permitted light and outside life to enter houses which were enclosed by unbroken walls without windows.

The city and the density of its population implied a complex organization; clearly state run. It had become impossible to govern such a large number of inhabitants and such vast conquered territories with the techniques left over from a tribal society. Moreover, the Teotihuacan society had affirmed its different social classes. Members of the lower classes —artisans or small-time merchants— lived in the districts, still linked by old family ties, and, if they were farmers, owning land in common. However at this time, the Teotihuacan districts were much more urban than rural, and they were grouped in every quarter of the city. The fact that there were four quarters was possibly a reminder of the ancient tribal division. Thus we have been able to distinguish three social and physical levels of organization. The smallest was formed by a family living in its house or apartment; the second is the district, made up of various families, and the third comprises each one of the four large sections of the city which include various districts. This social pyramid in three superimposed levels was crowned by the imperial society, pinnacle of the social structure: it retained the power, intellectual knowledge and priestly prestige.

But between this superstructure and the peo-

This *Zoomorphic decoration* on the sloping masonry encasements of the stairway still shows vestiges of the original polychromy that covered all Teotihuacan sculpture and architecture.

ple of the districts, there were three groups of people whose position is somewhat uncertain to us, although we know they were rather high up on the social scale. The first group was made up of merchants, not of the type who set up a modest stall on market-day, but those who undertook lengthy expeditions, who had dealings with foreing chieftains and traded in perishable goods. Possibly these astute merchants were given the task of collecting the taxes from the tributary nations.

The second group was composed of the militia, who rarely appear in the murals, despite their great importance. It has been said that

The *Pyramid of the Sun* seen from the *Pyramid of the Moon*. This is an example of religious character of buildings in Teotihuacan and Prehispanic Mexico in general. It covers an area similar to that of the Cheops Pyramid in Egypt, though it is not as tall.

Teotihuacan was a peaceful theocracy which governed a state where war was practically nonexistent. But although war, at that time,

does not seem to have been the chronic situation that it was later, it is unlikely that such a powerful state could have existed without an armed defense or that it could have expanded without relying on the army.

The priests formed the third and most important group. They were the guardians of enlightened culture and advanced knowledge. Apart from enjoying their religious role, they also directed the construction plans, indicat-

Anthropomorphic vessel in thin orange-colored earthenware, found in Xolalpan, which formed part of the ancient city of Teotihuacan (National Anthropology Museum).

ed the festival days and all the ceremonial rituals; they had to be experts in astronomy and mathematics in order to measure time and follow the calendar correctly. They were probably the only learned men who knew how to write and were in charge of the great mural compositions, which was why, among other reasons, the murals were nearly always related to religious themes. And religion was at the heart of everything. People from far and near did not come to Teotihuacan for merely commercial reasons, but because it had achieved fame for its impressive grandeur.

All this means that by then, there was already a complete civilization. Nevertheless, it is strange to note the almost total absence of writing, a very different situation from that of the Mayans and the peoples from Oaxaca.

INFLUENCE IN MESOAMERICA

Teotihuacan's influence became ever more powerful. It reached as far as Chiapas, and later, to Guatemala. It is very evident in sites such as Kaminaljuyu (where its great explorer, Dr. Kidder, thought that a virtual emigration of people from Teotihuacan had settled) and Tikal, where recent discoveries have revealed the presence of not only small Teotihuacan elements, such as figurines or vessels, but even Teotihuacan-style buildings, very different from the typical Mayan architecture and consequently easily distinguishable.

Teotihuacan mask, decorated with turquoise mosaic. This was found in Guerrero, which shows the extent of Teotihuacan's influence (National Anthropology Museum).

Teotihuacan sculpture with Olmec features, derived from the art of the Olmeccs, the oldest Mexican civilization.

What does this influence and expansion signify? How did it happen? What did it mean from the Teotihuacan point of view, that is, how can it help us to explain the evolution and stability of the urban city, and how did it reach the other places mentioned? We must examine two different situations here. The first is that of the metropolitan area, which included not only the city, but also the surrounding regions directly within the political empire and having the same culture. This covered at least the Mexico and Puebla valleys, part of the Tlaxcalan region and to some extent Hidalgo, mainly in the direction of Tulancingo (there is a possibility that this situation also ocurred in part of what is now the state of Morelos). At any rate, it is obvious that around Teotihuacan there is a very clear and very wide area in which we have found no remains from that era, other than those from the Teotihuacan world; there was no other local culture, although naturally, one finds the normal differences between a great city and a village, where certain things are not to be found.

On the other hand, in Veracruz, Oaxaca, Chiapas, Guatemala, and the West of Mexico, the situation is not the same. There, even though we find a strong Teotihuacan influence, it is an influence exerted over a local culture which did not lose its basic characteristics, although it did assimilate a great number of Teotihuacan elements. In exerting this influence, Teotihuacan demonstrates a totally imperialistic aproach. Imperial, of course, in the Mesoamerican sense, in which the important thing was to exact tributes, not only based on the army but also on commerce. If we exa-

Classic Teotihuacan mask worked in greenstone with shell teeth. The same material must have been used for the eyes.

Plumed serpent from the palace in Group 18 found north of the Quetzal-Butterfly Temple. It anticipates the great god Quetzalcoatl of the Toltec inheritors of Teotihuacan.

mine the commercial situation in the period with which we are better acquainted; that is, in the Aztec era, we can see that to the inheritors of the Teotihuacan world, commerce was a consequence of political action. When merchants launched forth beyond the frontiers of the Empire, it was because they went in a soldierly capacity. Thus there was a close link between the imperial militia and commercial expansion.

This Imperial expansion was neither total nor covered the entire territory but simply included isolated key points. It did not attempt to change the conquered governments nor take over their territory in a massive way. It simply attempted to forcibly impose a situation of demanding tributes so that the capital city could enjoy a leisurely life-style.

As part of the imperial expansion of Teotihuacan, it "exported" its religious ideology. With small regional differences we find that the gods of the various peoples were the same; they were Teotihuacan gods. Nevertheless, these peoples, when organizing their pilgrimages to the great city, took their gods with them together with their particular rituals which blended with Teotihuacan religious views. Thus, there was a profound religious-ideological exchange, in which it was the Teotihuacan cosmology that primarily asserted its characteristics and beliefs.

THE END OF METROPOLITAN TEOTIHUACAN

Teotihuacan IV

The following era, the phase which we call Teotihuacan IV, started about 600 A. D. and was still rich. But evidently, this is the phase in which the decline began. Gradually, certain buildings were abandoned. Some of the palaces begun to fall into ruin. It seems that they were not restored, or at least, no new frescoes were painted.

The temples, probably not all in use and perhaps partially abandoned, were not reconstructed when they fell. Everything points to a slow decadence, which made the city lose internal force, even though it still had a large population, possibly about 60,000 inhabitants, at least in the first part of this phase.

Even though Teotihuacan still controlled the Valley of Mexico and part of the Valley of Puebla, the city was slowly shrinking, but waves of other unorthodox and arrogant peoples began to emerge from the outskirts, bringing with them new problems. The decline was not only internal but also showed in the external relationships that constituted the empire, as a result of complex reasons which would be impossible to consider here.

Between 650 and 700 A.D., Teotihuacan was burned, invaded, plundered and partly destroyed. To this day traces of the last fire are clearly seen in many of the temples flanking the Avenue of the Dead, particularly in the Quetzalpapalotl. We do not know the reasons for this event which rocked Mesoameri-

Sculpture that may represent *the God of Death*. It can now be appreciated in the National Anthropology Museum.

ca, nor who was the main perpetrator of the offense, nor the causes which allowed it to happen. It is clear, however, that during the last years of its grandeur, Teotihuacan had begun to lose some of its metropolitan area, and more important still, it seems that the Valley of Puebla had been conquered by other people, which separated it from Teotihuacan hegemony. Therefore, due to lack of contact, relations broke altogether.

It is possible that the internal weakening of the city —without which its fall would be inexplicable— was due to the fact that within the bosom of the city lived various different groups, both local and foreign, who were not content to be subject to others. But there are

Earthenware representation of a *mortuary bundle*, indicating the Teotihuacan funerary customs.

Aerial view of the Avenue of the Dead Complex, with the street in the background, showing the architectural characteristics of the city's residential units.

indications that the main cause could have been the excessive centralization of all the power in the city, which caused the discontentment among the people of their rulers. The latter, who were the representatives of the gods on Earth, had once been a creative minority but had become an oppressive minority. The priests, once they had triumphed, thought only of preserving their power. At first they had given an enormous impulse to cultural and material achievements, accomplishing wonderful works of art, but now their inner strength fossilized, converting them into victims of the

first audacious person who would dare to attack the city.

The fall of Teotihuacan provoked a chain-reaction which must have also precipitated the fall of Monte Albán and of the great mayan culture during the 9 th. century. Its inhabitants emigrated to other regions, taking their culture with them, and they in turn formed new towns. The conquerors of Teotihuacan, installed in the ruins in vastly inferior conditions with adobe houses and mud floors —took numerous cultural features from Teotihuacan which eventually they passed on to the Mexicas. During this period of cultural acclimatization the newcomers forgot their true origins and, in a way very characteristic of Mesoamerica, they considered themselves not only as

The facade of the *Temple of Quetzalcoatl* in the Citadel is decorated with alternate representations of the plumed serpent, Quetzalcoatl and the rain god, Tlaloc. This remarkable example of Teotihuacan art was preserved for us by the fact that the entire facade was concealed within the new building when the Teotihuacan architects enlarged the platform.

descendents but as representatives of the past glory, since they had had the opportunity of living side by side with the few remaining inhabitants of Teotihuacan. From the mixture of both cultures developed the following period of the history of Mexico, which we call Toltecan.

THE LIVING MYTHICAL AND HISTORICAL TEOTIHUACAN

It is interesting to observe how history changes into myth, into a legendary past in which it was not men who created the great Teotihuacan, but giants, the gods themselves. This gave the name to these colossal ruins. Teotihuacan means, the place of the gods, or place where the gods were conceived. It is a posthumous naming, or at least a translation into *Nahuatl* from its original name which

In the hall dedicated to Teotihuacan in the National Anthropology Museum we can admire the *mural representing Tlalocan,* the paradise of the rain god, together with many other remarkable pieces from this great city.

has been lost to us, because we do not even know the language that was spoken there. Part of the deification process was told in the Fifth Sun legend.

In order to understand the significance of the suns and therefore, the Fifth Sun, one must think of the cyclical concept of history according to the indigenous mind. Unlike other histories, Mesoamerican history is not thought of as a linear system but starts with the creation of the Sun, the world, the animals, plants and men. At the end of a number of centuries, all creation was destroyed by a great cataclysm brought about by the gods. Then the cycle was repeated as the gods proceeded to a new creation. For the successors of Teotihuacan, this was the era of the Fifth Sun, as the previous four had died.

Serpent's head that decorated one of the sloping masonry encasements of a stairway. It still shows traces of its original coloring. It was discovered in

the most recent archaelogical excavations of Tectihuacan (1980-1982).

Patio of the Palace of the Quetzal-Butterfly with profusely carved pilasters. This stone carving is even more remarkable when we consider that the Teotihuacan people had no metal tools and that they carved with stone implements.

Bernardino de Sahagún (1500-1590) recorded the legend of the creation of this Fifth Sun when, at the death of the fourth sun, the world was in darkness. The Fifth Sun is that which illuminated the succesors of Teotihuacan and, now that we do not think of cyclical deaths, continues to shine on us. It is the Sun of the historic era.

The fact that this sun was created in Teotihuacan shows the prestige of the great city.

Its ruins are still a testimony of a vanished nation nevertheless protected by the gods. This prestige explains why Moctezuma II ordered a shrine built near the Pyramid of the Sun, where sacrifices were offered in honor of those gods who were so powerful that, though he was not aware of it, they were in fact the same as his gods. Teotihuacan was not only the first and greatest urban civilization we know of in Mexico, but it had also achieved developments never dreamed of before. It had elevated life and the organization of society to heights never before thought of. It was Teotihuacan that imposed, forever, its style of social and political life and its religious ideology.

In fact, all those who followed, whether Toltecs or Aztecs, were merely a variation of the Teotihuacan world. They copied the fundamental elements that Teotihuacan had left, naturally altering them and accommodating them to the new circumstances.

The whole indigenous civilization of the Plateau crystallized in Teotihuacan, which is what we have inherited and which through the historic proces has become part of the Mexican culture. Without the triumph of Teotihuacan, everything would have been different. The capital and center of Mexico probably would not have been on the Plateau at that terrible altitude, or 7,200 ft. If it is so, it is because Teotihuacan transformed this region into the geo-political center which the Mexicas called Anahuac, and which we, including a much greater area, call Mexico. This is why Teotihuacan history is the root of our history and continues to be valid.

ARCHAEOLOGY IN TEOTIHUACAN

The superb ruins of Teotihuacan were never lost to sight. They are mentioned several times by 16th. century and later chroniclers. But apart from the rather ingenuous archaeological attempt of Sigüenza, it seems that no one explored them until the 19th. century. There was considerable destruction whether intentional or not. A tremendous number of carved stones were re-used in the construction of houses or churches in the surrounding villages and a number of objects were discovered and unearthed by farmers. Likewise, unknown persons excavated many holes in search of treasure, such as those that Ramón Almaraz observed in the Pyramid of the Moon and other mounds in 1865. At the time, Almaraz published the first serious description based on

Unfinished Teotihuacan mask. We can see marks on it which give us an idea of the Teotihuacan sculptors' work techniques. (National Anthropology Museum).

direct studies of the ruins. At the turn of the century, Leopoldo Batres started excavations on a much larger scale: these have continued sporadically, with varying levels of activity, up to the present day. However, despite considerable advances and the wealth of material and information obtained about this ancient culture, only a fragment of the city has been scientifically explored.

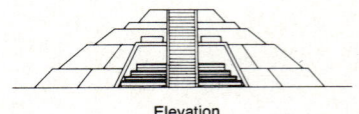

Elevation

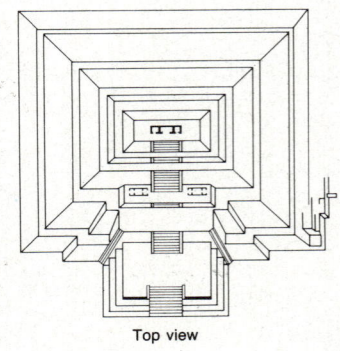

Top view

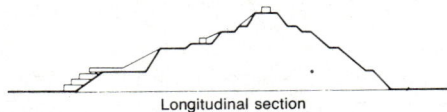

Longitudinal section

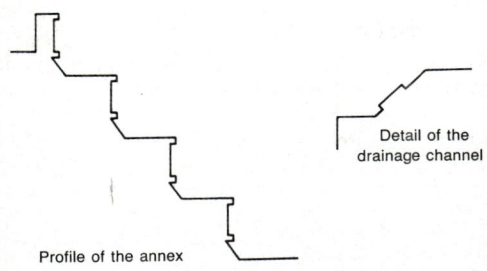

Detail of the drainage channel

Profile of the annex

The *Pyramid of the Moon* has a rectangular ground plan with a projecting body belonging to the original construction. *Above*: elevation, top view, and longitudinal section of the Pyramid of the Moon and profile of its annex.

A TOUR OF TEOTIHUACAN

The itinerary of a visit to Teotihuacan outlined in the following pages proposes that the visitor see all the most important points in the

Plaza of the Moon with the monumental volume of the *Pyramid of the Sun in the background.*

city. However, it may have the severe drawback of being too long for those who have insufficient time or the necessary stamina! It would take all day if one includes a lunch break and a rest wherever the visitor wishes.

The visitor with little time could shorten his tour according to his personal interests. The adjoining map shows the route.

THE MUSEUM

On arrival in the main parking area, we find some modern buildings, among which the museum is worthy of a brief visit. Here in synthesis are the principal elements that will help us to understand the development of the Teotihuacan culture whose capital we are going to visit. At the entrance is a replica of the colossal statue of the Goddess of Water, whose original the visitor may have seen in the National Anthropology Museum in Mexico City. It was transferred to Mexico City in 1885 and although it is not considered a great piece of sculpture, it does represent the typical geometric style of vertical and horizontal lines of the region.

Next, the first section of the Museum shows the location of Teotihuacan in space and time.

Monumental sculpture of the *Goddess of Water*, found in front of the Pyramid of the Sun and now in the National Anthropology Museum.

We can easily understand Teotihuacan's chronological relationship with other contemporary areas in Mesoamerica. At the same time we can appreciate the ecology of the region in relation to its geography and culture.

The other sections in this small museum attempt to explain the various aspects of Teotihuacan life and society, based on original objects, reproductions, models, pictures, and photographs. It is a preparation for the visit to the actual ruins and offers a better understanding of many existing but unseen aspects.

THE CITADEL

After visiting the museum, we will begin our tour of the great city with the impressive Citadel. This name is given to one of the greatest urban complexes of Teotihuacan. It comprises an enormous quadrangle with sides of 1,300 ft. made up of wide, elevated platforms at the top of which 15 smaller pyramids are symmetrically placed. Within the quadrangle, behind a splendid esplanade, rise two majestic temples as well as extensive dwelling areas distributed in harmonious symmetry.

The entrance to the so-called Citadel is by way of two wide stairways: the first leads from the level of the Avenue of the Dead to the top of the west platform and the second descends from it towards the Great Plaza. From the entrance platform, we can see the small temples that crown the four platforms that make up the Great Complex. Those found in the north, south and east are all oriented towards the center of this complex, whereas those that are situated on the entrance platform are oriented towards the Avenue of the Dead. From this same place, looking towards the interior, there is first a large open space that could accommodate 30,000 people. At

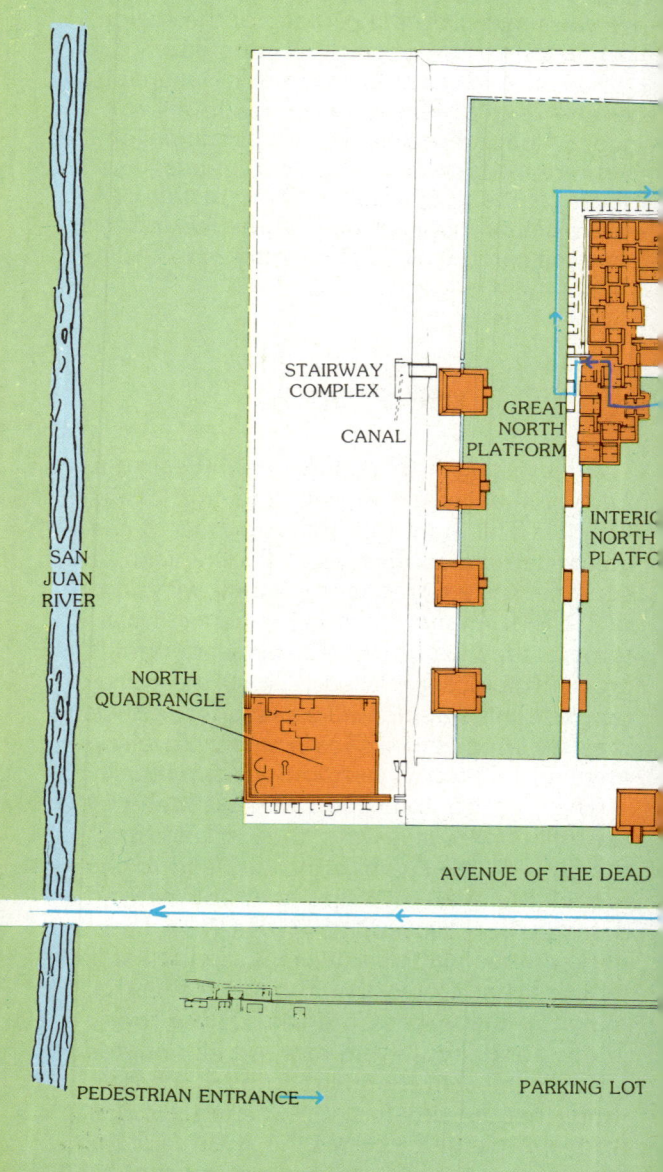

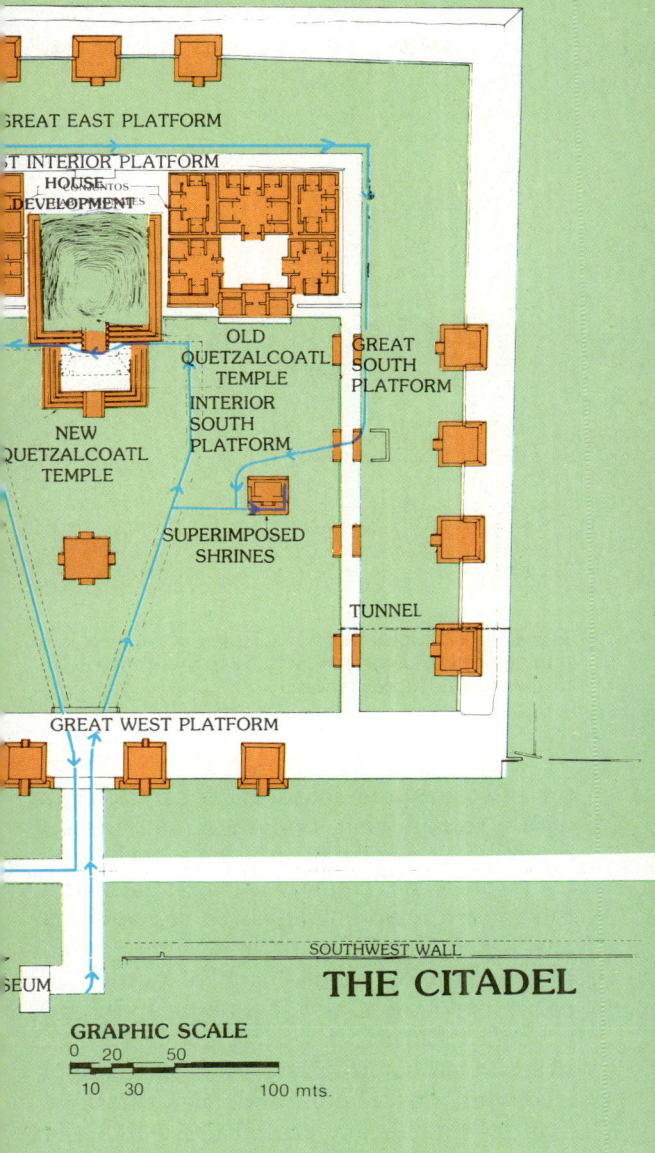

The Citadel, **monumental complex of temples and palaces. It is believed to have been the governmental center of Teotihuacan.**

the end of this great space, after a central shrine with a square base, one encounters one of the most important monuments of the city; the magnificent Temple of Quetzalcoatl. In fact, this refers to two buildings, one covering an earlier building. The more recent monument covering the older building displays the typical profile of the Classic Teotihuacan Period. It is composed of four sections of tablero-talud structure and a projecting central stairway. It is covered with cut stone and, like all the buildings of Teotihuacan, was finished with plaster painted in vivid colors with green circles on a red ground.

In order to view the older building, one enters from the south side by way of an opening with a modern finish which forms a narrow passage between the plastered building and the oldest pyramid. To the right one can admire what remains of the original completely sculpted facade. It was composed of a great central stairway on top of the seven terraced sections which formed the building. Today, there are only the lower four remaining, reduced from their original length by the superimposed building. The wide, sloping masonry enclosing the stairway is decorated with great serpent heads sculpted in the round, whose bodies undulate along their corresponding panels.

Like the main facade, all four sides were decorated in a similar fashion, entirely covered

Religious temples were dedicated to different gods. This stair platforms served as a basement to build those temples.

with beautifully carved stone. The protruding stones have large pegs which penetrate into the nucleus of the building, holding them in their correct position. On the relatively small *talud,* there are relief sculptures of long twisting serpents whose heads face towards the stairway. Judging by the conch-shells that appear between the undulations, the serpents are aquatic. Their bodies covered in feathers refer to Quetzalcoatl, the plumed serpent,

although more likely here associated with water than with the wind.

In this Temple of Quetzalcoatl, the wide tablero panels also have a serpentine nature again associated with conch-shells. However, the main decoration consists of a representation of two alternate elements. One of these is the head in the round of a serpent emerging from a kind of flower with eleven petals. This is another representation of Quetzalcoatl with his white painted, ferocious teeth and black, obsidian encrusted eyes. The second alternating figure is thought to represent Tlaloc, the rain god. However, some people think that

The plumed serpent, which has been identified as a representation of *Qetzalcoatl*. Its sinuous body glides across the framed panels of the platform (Temple of Quetzalcoatl).

it represents the same god that appears in Oaxaca from ancient times, who has been which classified in the urns of that region as "the god with the bow headdress" since his indigenous name is unknown. It is interesting to note that this is the only building in Teotihuacan in which we see two deities together. Generally, each

building seems to have been dedicated to the glory of one god only. All the panels are beautifully framed in stone cut with great precision, on which we can see green discs painted on a red ground. These represent "precious stones", symbols of jade.

From here we continue towards the North. On the way, we see an apartment compound which has been discovered recently. In order to get there one crosses a spacious porticoed platform whose flat roof was crowned by a parapet with merlons with the effigy of the god

Tlaloc. The roof is supported by lateral walls and thick pillars plastered and painted in red. Towards the center, this portico communicates with a large, square patio surrounded on each side by four rooms with their porticoes. Other sections and rooms grouped around private

The *God with the Bow Headdress,* whom some authors have identified as the rain god, Tlaloc. These large effigies alternate with those of Quetzalcoatl in the facade of the temple dedicated to this god.

patios are reached through narrow passages leading off this central patio at the heart of the complex. This is the classical distribution of the palaces and residential houses of Teotihuacan as we shall see further on in our tour through the City.

We walk to the upper part of the northern platform and we turn towards the east standing in the part behind the Citadel. In the short distance that we have come, we can view part of the ancient urban layout and note the precision of the axes which form the admirable

Detail of rattle in one of the representations of Quetzalcoatl, inspired by the rattlesnake, one of the most venomous serpents of Mexico.

symmetric plan of Teotihuacan. We see two enormous complexes of rooms and patios, one to the north and the other to the south of the Temple of Quetzalcoatl. Each of these similar complexes is regally conceived in an area of approximately 2 square acres. They are outstanding in the symmetry of their composition, the spaciousness of their areas, and the privacy with which some of the apartments are conceived. Each one consists of five sections communicated by passages and back courtyards through a large central distribution patio, which is the key element in each compound. This, in turn, is connected to the inner esplanade of the Citadel by way of two wide staircases and a porticoed room. The latter, due to its central position in the entrance, was the means by which there could be a strict control of access. It is thought that this was possibly the principal administrative center of the city.

Finally, before returning to the Avenue of the Dead, we will pause a moment to observe a small, but interesting shrine located towards the south side of the great esplanade. In the seven superimposed buildings of this small temple, the entire history of Teotihuacan from its first phase until its final stage is revealed.

THE AVENUE OF THE DEAD

Returning to the avenue of the Dead, we walk north. The street extends from this point for 1¼ miles towards the south but this part has not been explored. Going north, towards the Plaza of the Moon, there are another 1¼ miles, which means that the total length is 2½ miles. One should clarify that the name. "Avenue of the Dead" is incorrect. It was named by the Mexicas "Micaotli" because they thought that the buildings along it, already in ruins, were the sepulchral monuments of the kings and priests of Teotihuacan. While walking along the first section of the street between the Citadel and the entrance to the Plaza of the Moon, we will pass more than eighty platforms with the same proportions and in the same style. However, it is important to stress that what we now see is merely a small part of what this majestic sacred avenue must have been in its day.

One of the most recent explorers of Teotihuacan, René Millon, has written, "It is difficult to escape the conclusion that, by the Micaotli period (Teotihuacan II), if not sooner, the architects of the Avenue of the Dead purposely tried to amaze the visitor with the monumental size in concept of both the avenue and the pyramids and temples that flanked it. The later building of temples along the Avenue of the Dead and the Plaza of the Moon enlarged and emphasized this monumental concept. The majesty of the Plaza of the Moon is unrivalled

The *Avenue of the Dead* is the principal of the two axes that cross at right angles, around which the Teotihuacan urban plan developed.

in the prehispanic architecture of the New World. Also unrivalled is the enormous size of the Avenue of the Dead itself, the multitude of temples on top of the pyramids, and other structures on either side of the street, from the Plaza of the Moon up to the Citadel and the Great Complex. These last two gigantic areas apparently formed not only the symbolic center, but also the geographic, political and religious center of the City. Nothing approach-

ing the magnitude in concept is known in any other part of the Prehispanic New World. We cannot begin to understand something of the attraction, something of the magic and grandeur of Teotihuacan, if we do not recognize the consequences of the expression of monumentality in the general concept of the Avenue of the Dead. This grandeur and the rites that were performed in this setting must have caused a profound effect on many people, both from Teotihuacan and elsewhere. This must have charged the Teotihuacan religion with emotional and esthetic qualities which help to explain, at least in part, the attraction that it clearly held during so many years.

PLAZA 2

This Plaza is annexed to the Citadel along the full length of its northern *talud* and is on its west, north and east sides defined by a high wall from successive periods. Only a tenth part of it has been explored; this area, called the North Quadrangle, is located to the extreme west of Plaza 2 bordering on the Avenue of the Dead. Towards the street side, there is a series of rooms lined along the wall. They must have been residential areas judging by the large number of infant burials with offerings under the floors. However, due to their lineal distribution, they may have been commercial establishments to sell religious relics and objects. The entrance to this group was well controlled since there are only two narrow doors, one to the north of the Quadran-

The *Avenue of the Dead Complex* is one of the residential units of Teotihuacan and was probably occupied by the dominant social strata of the city.

gle and the other leading to the Avenue of the Dead. We will pass through the latter to visit the explored part.

After crossing the wall by a small door, one immediately sees two superimposed staircases on the right that lead from the middle platform of the Citadel to Plaza 2. Near these, to the northeast, we find a well dug in the rock with various cavities in its walls which served as steps for descent. Towards the end of a wide passage running along the north talud we find a strairway superimposed over a previous one of which little remains. This stairway has the peculiarity of not being superposed on the builing as was the usual practice in Teotihuacan. In fact, it is set into the large *talud*, forming the secondary entrance to the Citadel across the north platform.

The North Quadrangle is atypical within the urban distribution pattern, due to the fact that it shows buildings from different periods and especially because it was an area that played a special role in the economic, political and ideological aspects of Teotihuacan. It was here

that the religious and commercial ceramics were produced under the strict control of the groups who ruled the city from the Citadel. This complex is made up of various constructions, the most outstanding of which, because of their different shape, are the two semi-circular buildings thought to be the oldest in the city. There were various burials and offerings placed inside at a later date corresponding to the Teotihuacan Period III. A little to

The *Northwest Group* is another of the residential areas for the Teotihuacan elite. It borders on the Street of the Dead and is near the San Juan River, which the Teotihuacan people channeled in its course through the city.

the south of these semicircular buildings there is the silhouette of a small *temazcal* or steam bath of which only the foundations remain. The most recent constructions are the three symmetrically placed rooms in a Teotihuacan patio. These buildings are associated with the ceremonial ceramic workshops, because the thousands of pilgrims who came to the great city, returned with their sacred relics and objects.

THE NORTHWEST COMPLEX

On the west side of the Avenue of the Dead, after crossing the stream, there is another ar-

chitectural complex which has been recently excavated and is called the Northwest Complex of the San Juan River. This name was given because it is in fact situated in the northwest angle of the intersection of the Avenue of the Dead and the San Juan River. Its main entrance is approached from the street side, up two wide stairways which lead to a long platform with two medium-sized temples on top. These two temples are oriented towards the Avenue of the Dead and are similar to those one can see on the other side of the Avenue. One was destroyed in the construction of a road, but in the other we can distinguish two different construction periods.

From the entrance platform, we can view practically all of the excavated complex. In the foreground, after a wide passage in the front, are four large rooms symmetrically placed to the north and south of a wide porticoed area. These look out into a sunken patio surrounded by walkways. On three sides of this patio there are bases of pyramids and in the northeast and southeast corners of the complex various secondary rooms and patios are connected by narrow passages.

THE AVENUE OF THE DEAD COMPLEX

There is an enormous urban complex situated in the center of the Prehispanic city, planned around the Avenue of the Dead. This walled, nearly square area, is known as the "Avenue of the Dead Complex". The walls, some of them reaching a height of 7 ft., extend 383 yards in the east-west direction and 415 yds. in the south-north direction. It is

The *Pyramid of the Sun,* separated from the Avenue of the Dead by a large plaza. It was built in a single stage in the early times of Teotihuacan.

equidistant between the Pyramid of the Sun and the Citadel, that is to say, 274 yds. from its northern boundary to the southwest corner of the Pyramid of the Sun and the same distance from its southern boundary to the northwest corner of the Citadel.

The heart of this urban complex is a plaza situated on the Avenue of the Dead (the second plaza north of the San Juan River). This served as the main circulation area within the Great Complex. Its size is comparable to the Sun, Moon and Citadel complexes and is characterized by being a definite urban entity. It is made up of multiple urban areas and zones, which although varying in size, maintain the essential common pattern of three temples surrounding a plaza with its associated dwelling areas and their well-established internal communication system.

South of the Avenue of the Dead Complex, in which we see a patio surrounded by temples and dwellings.

THE SUPERIMPOSED BUILDINGS

A sign marks the entrance to the rear part of the Superimposed Buildings. After crossing through a wide, porticoed entrance, one first notices a patio surrounded by three temples; this is known as the Plaza of the Superimposed Temples.

The altar at the deepest level shows the *tablero-talud* system on its north-south and

east sides covered in plaster and decorated with geometric designs on the tablero in red, white and green, and on the molding a series of continuous frets. It is interesting to note that on the west face of this altar, which does not have a *tablero-talud*, there is a small bench with what looks like a built-in niche. In the upper part there is a small gutter which drains into the bench and then into another gutter in the floor.

We continue our tour going west from the Superimposed Temples and after climbing up one of the temple stairways, we can see two superimposed patios slightly to the north, demostrating different building periods.

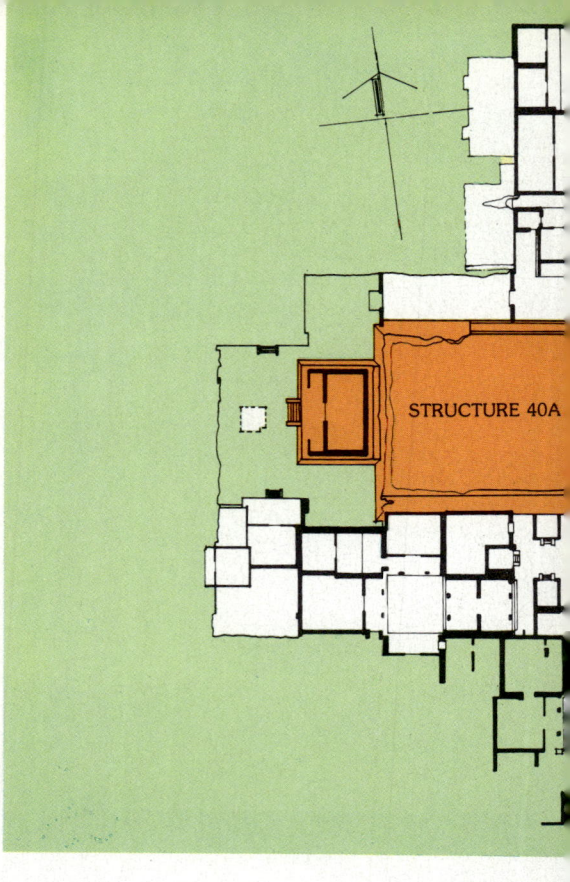

We now come to the constructions known as the Superimposed or Subterranean Buildings, which are some 65 ft. north of the Superimposed Patios. This name is not the most apt, because Teotihuacan is filled with superimposed buildings, these were the first to be discovered. What we find here are buildings from two periods that can be visited at the same time.

Among the rooms and patios at two levels, the most interesting thing to see is a temple painted all over with hooks.

Once again we find ourselves on the Avenue of the Dead which is the main axis and central artery of the City; strictly speaking, this is not a street but the area that joins a series of oblong plazas, joined one with the other by stairs

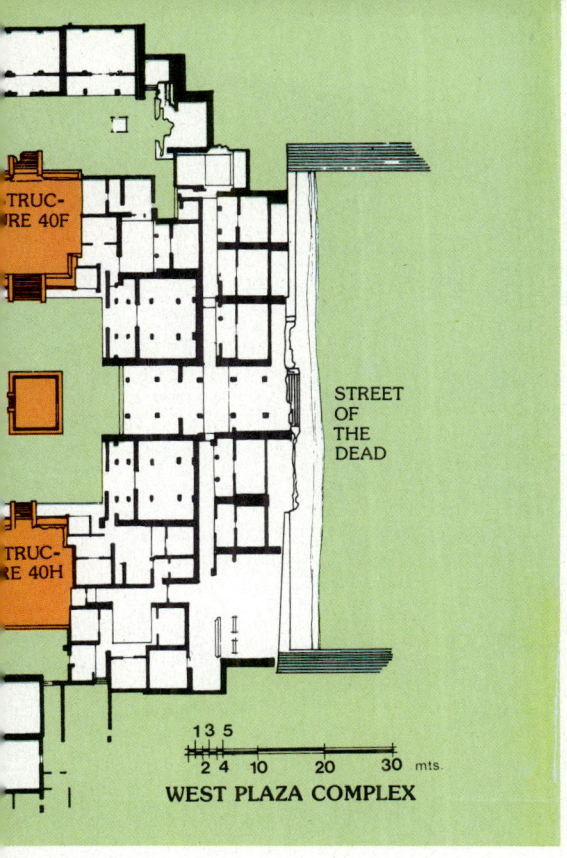

which the 98 ft. elevation difference from the Citadel to the Plaza of the Moon necessitated. These steps were essential because each group of buildings was situated on a flat piece of ground and they help to give a pleasing perspective view. Furthermore, the natural slope of the land allowed a series of open drainage ditches to be built which flowed into what we could call a central water conduit along the Avenue of the Dead.

Almost directly in front of the Superimposed Buildings, across the street, there is another group known as the "1917 Excavations". This group, partially excavated, displays the foundations of temples surrounded by patios and dwellings.

Square from West Plaza Complex, another one of the various located along the Street of the Deads. A shrine in the center of the square was a common disposition in teotihuacanian architecture.

THE WEST PLAZA COMPLEX

The visitor should go through the original entrance from the Avenue to tour this group of buildings in the Avenue of the Dead Complex. It is the largest and most complete group

so far explored. From here we climb the stairway which leads to the top, whose west side faces the street. At this level, there is series of rooms flanking a spacious, porticoed area in the center which is the only controlling access for the entire complex. On going through the portico, we find ourselves at a junction; two narrow passages leading to other sections of this group head north and south from this point. Further on, we come to another elegant, porticoed room which provides a direct entrance to the central zone. There we find a spacious, rectangular patio (75 × 101 ft.) with a shrine in the center. On the north and south sides there are twin temples formed by double sections of stairs and on the west side is an impressive temple whose stairway encasements were decorated with jaguar heads.

We can see a sequence of two constructive periods here; the distribution of space at both

Viking Group near the Pyramid of the Sun, in which we see a repetition of the architectural elements common in the residential areas of Teotihuacan.

levels is similar. Obviously the oldest construction is to be found at the greater depth and it is here that we can see part of the main temple and central shrine. Two outstandingly beautiful serpent heads are integrated into the temple; by their positioning, they transmit the same idea of the serpent heads that adorn the masonry encasements of the famous Quetzalcoatl Temple in the Citadel. That is, according to the information we have, these enormous monolithic sculptures must have been incrusted all along the masonry stairway encasements, supported by their forked tongues on the surface. However, during the building

of the next level, they were dismantled from their original position leaving only the two heads that we see now.

Returning again to the most recent construction period, we can see that on the four corners of the enormous central patio, there are entrances to passages and porticos which communicate with other sections of the compound. Here we see sunken patios, porticoed elements, supports, shrines, vestibules, a complete sewer system with its drains, gutters, etc., examples of monumental structures built into the architecture and even an example of mural painting. From a structural point of view, it is worth noting a series of typical Teotihuacan elements, such as the reinforced talud walls sloping at the bottom or the walls strengthened by the addition of pillars, the internal wooden reinforcing; the vertical and horizontal molding which form the classical *tablero-talud*, the doorframes, etc.

THE VIKING GROUP

Continuing up along the street, we come to the Viking group which was named after the foundation that sponsored its partial excavation. It extends 270 ft. along the street and comprises a group of porticoes, rooms, courtyards and shrines around an open-air patio. It is all in typical Teotihuacan style with one curious exception: under the ground of one of the interior patios there is a floor, nearly 322 feet square, which is made of layers of mica sheets. It is incredible that it such a fragile material would have been used as a floor to walk on, which leads us to believe that it had some ceremonial use.

THE PLAZA OF THE SUN

On continuing our walk along the street, we pass two stairways which lead up to the next platform. These appear as open spaces because they have not been excavated. They surely contain other monuments. The last and highest of these small plazas is precisely in front of the Pyramid of the Sun, whose inmense mass we see to our right.

THE PYRAMID OF THE SUN

We immediately notice that a spacious plaza separates the pyramid from the avenue. Without going in, or visiting them in detail, we can observe a series of buildings that form various groups.

Almost in the street, there is a small structure whose importance is that it is not from the Teotihuacan culture. It is a shrine and the remains of low platforms from the Aztec era built some seven hundred years after Teotihuacan. It is said, that occasionally Moctezuma II used to come here to pray to those omnipotent gods who built Teotihuacan.

The pyramid is surrounded by a high platform, except on the west side, which forms a street between the pyramid and the platform. This joins the plaza in front of the pyramid which in turn communicates with the Avenue of the Dead by two steps. The remains of eight platforms exist within the plaza. These are distributed in a regular way and form small groups around rectangular patios.

On the platform, to the south, we see the structure called the "Priests' House", consisting of several small patios surrounded by rooms which are connected by passages.

The other buildings around the pyramid are arranged on the platform in a U-shape open to the street. The platform has been partially restored on the south side. Crossing over the plaza from west to east, we see a central shrine typical of the indigenous plazas.

Once we have crossed over the Plaza of the Sun, 229 ft. wide, we stand in front of the gigantic mass of the monument itself. A few years ago a natural cave slightly more than 328 ft. long was discovered. It ended in a chamber shaped like a four-petaled flower. Through the years, the long subterranean passage was closed off by various walls, until it was entirely covered. A well, 23 ft. deep, which led to the cave, was filled in with stones and dirt. The important thing is that the cave lies almost exactly in the center of the pyramid, underneath the upper platform. This indicates that the pyramid itself, which is the largest in

The Pyramid of the Sun, a magnificent example of the grandeur of the Teotihuacan culture, which so greatly influenced other regions of Mesoamerica.

Teotihuacan, was originally built in relation to the cave and therefore must have been particularly venerated.

The pyramid comprises two buildings: the actual pyramid and the monument attached to it in front of the plaza; this is much smaller and of course of a later date.

The pyramid itself is undoubtedly the largest in Precolumbian America. It measures 738 ft. on each side and is approximately 213 ft. high. Including the temple which no longer exists on its summit, it would have reached about 249 ft.

In the first important excavation carried out by Batres at the beginning of this century, the four sides were discovered. By a mistake, understandable at the time, the excavator shaved off about 23 ft. of three sides of the last superimposed construction. Only the main façade on the west retains its original size. Owing to the reduction, the terraced walls seen today were originally buttresses or retention walls that were, of course, hidden under the

final layer that covered the original structure. At one time, the entire pyramid was covered with a thick layer of smooth plaster. This served as a decorative device and was painted all over, probably in red. Inside the pyramid is a much smaller monument built over the cave.

The pyramid as it stands today, besides the adjoining monument at the front, is composed of five terraced sections built of clay and stone with a final finish. Four of the sections have only a *talud,* but the fourth from the bottom, the shortest section, also has a *tablero.* Unlike the other buildings, this does not have a continuous stairway from the base to the top; rather, each section has its own flight of stairs. It would have been difficult to build one single stairway because of the enormous height.

There was probably a sculptured stone decoration on the facade of the building attached

Small temples crowning the platforms on either side of the Street of the Dead, in front of the Pyramid of the Sun.

to the pyramid, similar to one on the Quetzalcoatl Temple, since important pieces of it have been found in one of the most recent excavations. Unfortunately, they were so destroyed that it was impossible to restore the stones to their original position.

FOUR SMALL TEMPLES

On returning to the avenue, we see the Four Small Temples a few paces to our left. They acquired this name due to the fact that there are four temples, symetrically erected on a low platform. Looking to our right, a little further on, we will notice a 656 ft. wall that hides a series of Teotihuacan style foundations, and which unfortunately breaks the rhythm and majestic unfolding of the avenue. This wall was built after the fall of Teotihuacan or in its last moments, possibly by the Chichimecas

or whoever destroyed the city and afterwards settled in parts of it. Lamentably few traces remain of an enormous mural painted on the side facing the wall. It depicts a gigantic jaguar walking in profile towards the south.

MYTHICAL ANIMALS

Other interesting paintings were found in the next building across the avenue. This is the group known as the Mythical Animals. The structure is quite low and has two terraced sections with a stairway in its axis. The earliest of the two construction periods partially existing is the most interesting. In order to visit it and its frescoes, one must go around the building and enter by a modern entrance at the back of the complex. Here is a room completely decorated with numerous figures that could be considered miniatures. They still retain their vivid colors, predominantly green,

Jaguar in one of the murals from the Mythical Animals building. It has faded with the passage of time and is now difficult to see. The jaguar appears frequently in Teotihuacan and Mesoamerican symbolism.

blue, yellow and red. All the frescoes in Teotihuacan must have been painted in these basic brilliant colors. Obviously, the majority have faded with time and today we can hardly see them. Here are depicted: fighting animals, plumed serpents (reminding us of Quetzalcoatl), jaguars in varying positions, winged fish which look more like doves, and saurians (a type of lizard) which display large protuberances in their bodies. One jaguar is devouring a fish-bird; another feline, oddly painted green with black spots, appears to be scratching its back. An impressive plumed serpent head emits a stream of water from its mouth, while two other strange, ferocious animals appear to be on the verge of devouring one another. All this takes place in the water which we can distinguish because of the lines in the background of the composition.

TEMPLE OF AGRICULTURE

Next, we encounter the Temple of Agriculture which forms an angle with the Plaza of the Moon. It exhibits several clearly defined periods, the oldest one represented by a platform some 26 ft. in height. Later, the Teotihuacan architects superimposed a series of modifications that are difficult to distinguish, but which generally follow similar architectural elements seen in other buildings. The explorer Leopoldo Batres discovered two important paintings at the back of the monument. These were not properly protected but happily, have been preserved in fairly accurate copies. The most interesting one is a complex scene in which a series of individuals appear to be carrying offerings towards two smoking braziers.

The other painting, which gives its name to the building, is an enormous composition made up of three murals. In them, there appear the water symbol, conch-shells, flowers, fruit, sheaves of feathers, and, probably from

a later date, a hieroglyph painted in the center. One can still distinguish it even though it is in fairly bad condition.

THE PLAZA OF THE MOON

We continue our tour with the Plaza of the Moon, which represents the supreme triumph of the Teotihuacan architecture and urbanism. Here the size, proportions, and distribution of the buildings which surround it, the pyramidal bulk and the attached structure achieve a unity perhaps only rivalled in Mesoamerica by the Plaza of Monte Alban in Oaxaca.

Here, we have the advantage that nearly all the elements were reinforced and well-reconstructed in recent years, with the exception of the upper temples that were lost through

The *Plaza of the Moon* serves to frame the great Pyramid, and the Street of the Dead ends in this monumental complex.

the destruction of time. This gives us not only wonderful impression, but also a fairly accurate one of what it must have been like. Of course one should not forget that all the buildings were finished in painted plaster. Today we only see the ochre colored stone.

The Plaza of the Moon measures 669 × 449 ft., and is surrounded by wide, terraced platforms very similar to each other. Together, they give the impression of monumentality and splendid planning. As we mentioned before, all the constructions are missing their upper most temples. However, at the bases there are some esthetically poor room constructions. These were added centuries later.

As one crosses the middle of the plaza in the direction of the pyramid, the visitor will come acroos a square altar. This is decorated on all sides with panels and staircases and must have been where the ceremonies and dances took place. These would have been seen by the multitudes crowded in the square and on the steps of the stairways that surrounded the monuments.

The *Pyramid of the Moon* is the second largest building in Teotihuacan, although it has not yet been completely restored. Its back part shows what these huge buildings were like before the archaeological explorations began at the end of the 19th century.

THE PYRAMID OF THE MOON

Almost at the foot of the Pyramid of the Moon, a little further on, we see a strange building decorated on its four sides by panels. The only entrance is on the west side. Inside are ten small altars, nine attached to the walls and one in the center. We do not know of any other similar arrangement in Mesoamerica, nor do we know exactly what its purpose was. However, its position indicates that it must have been of considerable ritual importance.

With this we arrive at the building attached to the pyramid. It is in the beautiful classical Teotihuacan style and is made up of five terraced sections, reaching a height of 56 ft. Where these sections join the pyramid, there are two sloping open drains coming down from the upper platform.

The Pyramid of the Moon occupies the whole north side of the plaza and reaches 152 ft. in height. It is therefore much smaller than the Pyramid of the Sun, but as it was built on higher ground, its upper platforms are in fact at the same height above sea level. The difference is in the gradient, which we will notice while walking up the Avenue of the Dead. Only the first three sections have been partially reconstructed, since the fourth has been left as it was found in the excavation. These large sections are in *talud*, but do not have *tableros*. One ascends by way of an enormous stairway which is divided into four flights. This magnificent monument must have had tremendous ritual importance.

THE PALACE OF THE QUETZAL-BUTTERFLY

Descending once more to the plaza, we head towards the extreme southwest where the Palace of the Quetzal-Butterfly (Quetzalpapalotl) and its related buildings are situat-

Patio in the Palace of the Quetzal-Butterfly, one of the few buildings around the Plaza of the Moon that did not function as a temple.

ed. Here follows a summary of the description given by archaeologist Jorge Acosta: A group of buildings known as the Palace of the Quetzal-Butterfly is in the southern corner of the plaza. This magnificent palace was discovered in 1962 and, although it was found tumbled down, all the necessary architectonic elements existed for its reconstruction which was accomplished successfully.

First one goes up a wide stairway, decorated on the north side with an enormous serpent head. The upper part opens onto an elegant portico with thick columns and completely roofed over. It displays a painted mural with apparently abstract motifs. The upper part of the walls is decorated in red.

Turning northeast we descend through a small door to an open patio surrounded by thick columns completely decorated on three sides with lovely bas-reliefs. In the middle of each support, one can see the figure of the mythological animal known as "Quetzal-

Bas-relief of a quetzal bird on one of the columns in the Palace of the Quetzal-Butterfly, from which it derives its name.

Butterfly" (a well known god in Teotihuacan), with a series of symbols, all related to water, placed above and below in horizontal borders. The motifs on the west side are somewhat different for here a bird (quetzal?) appears, with extended wings viewed from the front.

Originally, the bas-reliefs were polychromed like everything else and some of the symbols were inlaid with obsidian, although the back of each column is undecorated. Many of these reliefs can still be appreciated *in situ*.

At the base of the walls, there are some interesting mural paintings, those in the north being the best preserved. Red was used as the background color for a series of geometrically stepped shapes, which represent the cross-section of a sea-snail shell. Elegant merlons, with the Teotihuacan year sign, rise from the top parapet that runs round the entirely restored patio.

This sumptuous palace contains the three largest rooms so far discovered in Mesoamerica. Each side measure 26 ft. and surprisingly, they lack any center support.

Undoubtedly this was a great king's or high priest's residence, since as such, he would have to be surrounded by luxuries worthy of his high rank.

THE JAGUAR PALACE

Leaving the Palace of the Quetzal-Butterfly, we pass through the portico and then through a door in the southeast angle. After going down a narrow staircase, we walk along one of the old Teotihuacan streets which takes us past a series of rooms to a great rectangular patio. It has a double sectioned platform and chambers surrounding it on the north, south and west sides, while there is a narrow staircase in the center of the east side. It is interesting to mention, that at the base of each support

Patio of the Jaguar Palace, which may have been occupied by high-ranking priests.

there is an embedded vertical stone, representing a snake's rattle.

This patio with its side rooms, which are more like individual apartments, has been called the Jaguar Palace, owing to the number of feline representations which appear on the lower walls. In the northeast corner of the patio is a passage which leads to another group of rooms more to the north. One of these contains an interesting and unusual mural painted on a white ground, in which one can observe pairs of human hands carrying small felines wrapped in a kind of net and from their

mouths issue huge curved shapes representing their roar.

Three chambers border on the north side the great patio. In the central chamber there are some paintings that are still in magnificent condition and show two identical jaguars on either side of the door. Each wears a large feathered headdress and is adorned from the back to the tip of the tail with a string of shells. They are blowing on a conch-shell which they hold in the front paw. The musical instrument is decorated with feathers and from the front emerges the sound symbol in two curved shapes dripping drops of blood. These figures are framed by a border containing representations of Tlaloc alternated with the year symbol. The composition is related to rain and fertility.

Before leaving this complex which was in use simultaneously with the Palace of the Quetzal-Butterfly, we should mention that complicated system of concealed drains exists, running underneath the rooms and patios, and small holes in the floors lead to the sewers. Some of these are found in covered rooms, probably bath rooms.

SUBSTRUCTURE OF THE PLUMED CONCH-SHELLS

Under the Palace of the Quetzal-Butterfly is a group of older, subterranean structures which can be visited by way of a modern tunnel located in the previous patio. This is a series of facades, each linked to the next, of which the most important is the Temple of the Plumed Conch-shells. It is perhaps one of the most

Plumed jaguars carrying a musical instrument made from a conch-shell. These murals provided the name by which this temple is known.

beautifully balanced architectonic structures ever realized in Teotihuacan.

It was built between the 2nd and 3rd. centuries after Christ and was partially destroyed and filled-in intentionally to create an enormous platform on top of which the palace of the Quetzal-Butterfly was to be built.

The bas-relief representations of large shells decorated with feathers which we see on its facade gave its name later to the temple. As each has a kind of mouthpiece, we suppose that they were musical instruments. What particularly attracts our attention are the two slender columns placed on either side of the structure. These are decorated with bas-reliefs of four-petalled flowers. Both these and the previ-

Bas-relief portraying feathered conch-shells belongs to an older building over which the Palace of the Quetzal-Butterfly was built.

ous motifs are painted in various colors which stand out against a brick-red background.

The temple stands on a low platform decorated with panels where one can distinguish numerous green birds (parrots?). From their yellow beaks spring streams of blue liquid mixed with symbols that look like eyes. Various odd drops splash from this stream.

A small tunnel goes west from the structure's axis and penetrates as far as an ancient temple. This still displays part of a shrine or altar in a perfect state of preservation. Its only decorations are plain red circles on a white ground, which we know symbolize the "most precious".

We should mention that at the time the most ancient buildings were in use, the ones above, of course, did not exist, and therefore the older ones were out in the open, with their respective roofs.

This most interesting group of buildings concludes our visit to the ceremonial area of Teotihuacan in what we might call the center of the city.

Now we will visit some of the city palaces that have been excavated in the outlying areas. Many more undoubtedly exist but they have not yet been investigated.

TEPANTITLA

The name means "place of standing walls" and it is found approximately ¼ mile east of the Pyramid of the Sun, near the Number 2 parking lot. The excavations in these ruins indicate that they must have been the remains of a priest's house, like many that existed around the ceremonial center. As we go in, we notice some of the restoration necessary to protect the murals adequately. Most of them are merely fragments but in the covered patio we can discern how it was once entirely painted with scenes. We reach the patio by crossing the main square of the house, where a small corridor on the right leads us to it. At the back and to either side of the door, we

The original *Tlalocan Mural in Tepantitla.*

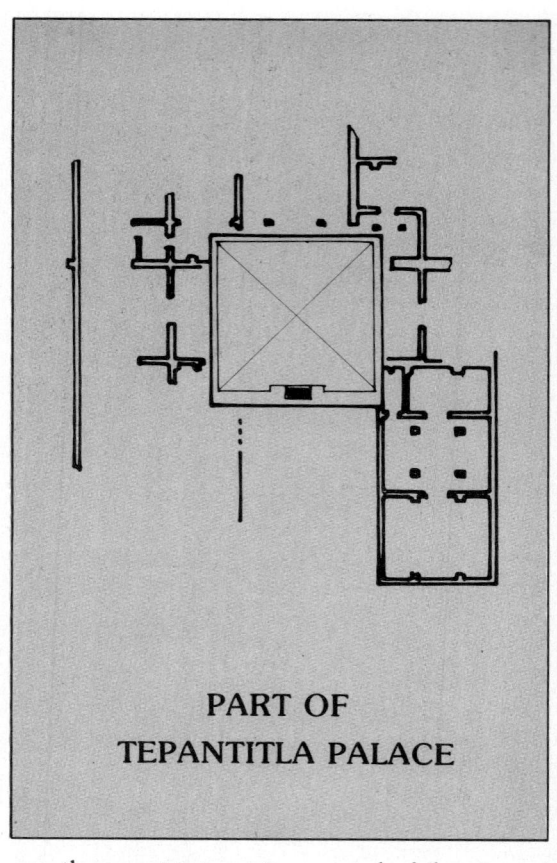

PART OF TEPANTITLA PALACE

see the most interesting mural of the group. Although it is in rather bad condition, it is by far one of the most fascinating in Teotihuacan (Fortunately we have an exact copy in the National Antrhropology Museum).

Each of the two sections divided by a central door is presided over by a divine presence: that of the god Tlaloc. He is sumptuously and allegorically adorned and allows drops of rain to fall on the earth. On either side of Tlaloc is a luxuriously dressed priest walking towards the god. As he walks, he lets seeds and jade beads fall to the ground from his hands. A curved object symbolizing speech, which in this case must have been a magic spell since it is decorated with flowers, also issues from his hands. Tlaloc wears a huge headdress in the shape of the quetzal bird with two trees growing from its spread wings. There are butterflies in the branches of one of the trees and spiders in the other. At the center of the composition is a spider hanging by a thread. The face of the god is covered by a mask through which his eyes appear. The mouth is covered with a plate bearing five fangs on top of the forked tongue of a serpent decorated with starfish. These are the large figures which form the priestly motif of the fresco.

In the most unusual part of the painting, to the lower right, appears what Alfonso Caso interprets as a representation of Tlalocan, in other words, the paradise of Tlaloc, the god of water. To the lower middle, we see a great river flowing to both sides from a blue mountain. But judging by the people swimming in it, the mountain is all water. There are also aquatic animals, plants and fish in it. This mountain and its river, like the rest of the mural, must symbolize a true paradise.

The whole composition is of a delightful garden filled with flowers, plants, birds and butterflies. Only one figure to the extreme right does not join in the fun; large tears fall from his eyes.

The importance of this fresco lies beyond its esthetic value, for it is one of the rare documents in which the painter expresses a philosophy of the Teotihuacan man. Here he expresses his yearning for the ideal that he could never achieve in life but hoped to enjoy after death; the idyllic paradise, the place of delights, where all his longed for desires, which were frequently frustrated in real life, would be attained. We notice that only one woman is represented here, which leads us to deduce a lack of sexual interest. Neither is there the least desire to beautify the human body. It shows a simple world of almost childish pleasures with children's games. Obviously the cen-

Detail of the Tepantitla mural which represents Tlaloc's paradise. Numerous men play, sing, and dance in an idyllic place which has an abundance of water, flowers and plants.

tral theme is the exuberance of nature at the time when the god deigns to send the refreshing water necessary to renew life.

On the left side of the door, we see an open ground where many little human figures, almost identical in style to those on the other side, are seen involved in a ball game in which sticks are used, while they sing. The standing stelae probably mark the edge of the playing field. This ball game is quite different from others known elsewhere.

In both paintings the artist does not follow the official regulations of the great compositions except in the upper part where the religious themes are interpreted using their rigid rules. However, in the lower part the artist lets his imagination run wild and freely depicts human desires in a spontaneous and natural art. In this sense, this composition is unique among the numerous Teotihuacan frescoes.

Still in Tepantitla, in another room, there are representations of luxuriously dressed priests in different shades of red. In yet another room we can vaguely see a procession of priests dressed in their pompous finery with the highly decorated speech symbol flowing from their hands instead of their mouths.

ATETELCO

On leaving Tepantitla one must go by car along the cobbled road circling west of the city. Just before reaching the San Juan River, a narrow dirt road leads west towards the *Barrio de Purificación*. There is a sign pointing to two places, Tetitla and 400 yards further on, Atetelco. We will visit the latter first and see Tetitla and other palaces worth visiting on our return.

The name Atetelco means "on the stone wall by the water" and there are two reason for visiting it. The first is that the quantity of murals is unsurpassed in any other region and the other, more important reason is that here we acquire much more information on the residences of both the Teotihuacan elite and of other groups, probably families. These continued to live side by side in separate apartments with a communal altar or shrine. The size and perfect proportions of the dwellings and their patios are truly impressive. Their drainage systems are also very interesting, though concealed. We do not know of any other such elaborate and spacious houses in the Mexican Plateau.

Today only the bottom part of the walls remain, except where the walls have been restored to their original height so that a roof could be built to protect the murals beneath.

Atelelco consists of two patios surrounded by apartments. On entering the first and most recent one, we observe the typical, square patio of a large Teotihuacan house. The four recessed corners each form a patio. Each side has a staircase with masonry encasements. In the center is a small reconstructed shrine, with three small *taluds* and their corresponding low *tableros* in keeping with the total height of the shrine. It was painted all over with narrow horizontal stripes in red and turquoise.

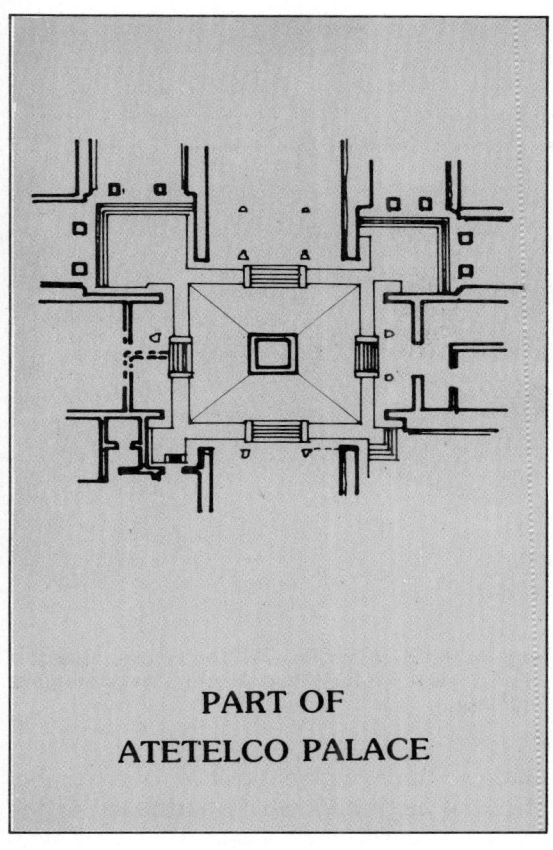

PART OF ATETELCO PALACE

Unfortunately, practically nothing remains, but a reconstruction was worked out on paper. A miniature temple rests on top of the shrine with a recess facing west. The decoration is completed with a series of stone merlons surrounding it. One can find a few traces of paintings in both the south room of the patio and different parts of the interior walls. Evidently, it was originally decorated all over. One of the porticoes has the half square and half rounded columns which are a characteristic feature of Teotihuacan.

The following patio has been named the White Patio and is the oldest. It is surrounded by three porticoes that have been reconstructed up to roof height. This permitted the resto-

Patio in the Atetelco Palace. **The central altar is a small-scale reproduction of the city's large religious buildings.**

ration to their original position of a number of mural fragments which had fallen to the ground when the ancient walls were destroyed.

The missing parts have been repainted, but the original is clearly distinguishable from the modern parts. A sloping border on two of the porticoes is decorated with jaguar figures, or perhaps coyotes, with a large feathered headdress. From their half-open mouths emerges the sound symbol, as though they were roaring. Underneath there is a hieroglyph which may signify the heart, from which fall three drops of blood. At the top part of the interior portico walls is a decoration of diamond shapes forming a net. A priestly figure laden with feathers and ornaments is shown in each diamond. Despite the similarity between the three porticos, the figures are different. That is, the priests in the south carry a bird's head, those in the east seem to be dedicated to the cult

of Tlaloc, while those in the north are related to the coyote. The richness of each grouping is enhanced by the frames of the paintings, the net-like mesh and the doors, also decorated with various motifs.

Going out to the north portico, we see a curious human figure with bodily deformations, on either side of the doorjamb. One of them has his feet twisted inwards; the other shows a deformed foot. In the indigenous world there was considerable interest in deformed beings, dwarfs, hunchbacks, and those stricken with illnesses that marked the body. Perhaps they refer to Nanahuatzin who, according to the legend of the suns, was a carbuncle-afflicted individual who turned into the sun.

TETITLA

After visiting Atetelco, it is worthwhile to continue on to Tetitla which is only some 400 yards to the west. Its name means "place of stones". It is an enormous, complex accumulation of patios, porticoes, residences and corridors, from at least two periods. The complex is divided into several very irregular sections which suggest separate houses and not the residence of one great leader. However, they are all joined into one large building which takes up an entire block. It is surrounded by typical Teotihuacan streets which can be seen in detail here and in the nearby palaces. The houses are enclosed by long, windowless walls, only broken here and there by doors with steps leading to the interior of the dwellings.

On the other hand, the high walls enclosing the structures in each block do give the impression of an easily defendable fortress. A coat of plaster covered these outside walls, the same as on the interior walls.

If Tetitla is impressive for its size, it is even more so for its extraordinary abundance of painted murals. It is impossible to describe each patio or each group which the visitor can easily reach, much less mention every fresco. There are no fewer than 120 painted walls,

The eagle, another animal charged with symbolism in the Prehispanic era, is depicted in one of the remarkable mural paintings in the Tetitla Palace.

some of which are still in quite good state, while others are left only a few traces. In some ways, this is the painting gallery of Teotihuacan.

Here we see the richly dressed gods, sometimes throwing gifts to the earth; the numerous animals, among which the most conspicuous are the jaguars with their plumed headdresses of various associated symbols, serpents and birds, quetzals or owls in the moment of alighting with their wings spread; human figures among the waves, represented by wavy blue lines, similar to those we saw in the Mythical Animals fresco; interesting "abstract" paintings which may represent a building, and many more.

The portico east of the main patio —which has a central shrine representing a Teotihuacan temple on its platform with a stairway entrance— displays six large feathered felines resting on a kind of low bench. Near the open mouth of the animal, we have a three-lobed motif in red over half moons in white. The felines are painted in orange with blue eyes.

The architectonic motifs mentioned before are repeated in the south portico but they show a unique characteristic: the lines are marked in white. In the west portico of this same patio, there are large, frontal view figures of priests in ceremonial attire. An enormous headdress of quetzal feathers has a bird's head at the center. The priests' faces are covered by jade masks and they wear large, round earrings of the same material. The rest of the vestments are very opulent and from their extended hands, jade gifts fall to the ground, signifying drops of water to the world. This is a feature we have noticed in other places. Their red-painted nails demonstrate the interest that Teotihuacanos had in the hands, and as always, they had not forgotten to show the nails. Moreover, in this case, the hands are placed